D1524573

Reindeer

by Rebecca Pettiford

BLASTOFF! READERS
2

BELLWETHER MEDIA • MINNEAPOLIS, MN

Note to Librarians, Teachers, and Parents:

Blastoff! Readers are carefully developed by literacy experts and combine standards-based content with developmentally appropriate text.

Level 1 provides the most support through repetition of high-frequency words, light text, predictable sentence patterns, and strong visual support.

Level 2 offers early readers a bit more challenge through varied simple sentences, increased text load, and less repetition of high-frequency words.

Level 3 advances early-fluent readers toward fluency through increased text and concept load, less reliance on visuals, longer sentences, and more literary language.

Level 4 builds reading stamina by providing more text per page, increased use of punctuation, greater variation in sentence patterns, and increasingly challenging vocabulary.

Level 5 encourages children to move from "learning to read" to "reading to learn" by providing even more text, varied writing styles, and less familiar topics.

Whichever book is right for your reader, Blastoff! Readers are the perfect books to build confidence and encourage a love of reading that will last a lifetime!

This edition first published in 2019 by Bellwether Media, Inc.

No part of this publication may be reproduced in whole or in part without written permission of the publisher. For information regarding permission, write to Bellwether Media, Inc., Attention: Permissions Department, 6012 Blue Circle Drive, Minnetonka, MN 55343.

Library of Congress Cataloging-in-Publication Data

Names: Pettiford, Rebecca, author.
Title: Reindeer / by Rebecca Pettiford.
Description: Minneapolis, MN : Bellwether Media, Inc., 2019. |
    Series: Blastoff! Readers. Animals of the Arctic | Audience: Age 5-8. |
    Audience: K to Grade 3. | Includes bibliographical references and index.
Identifiers: LCCN 2018030992 (print) | LCCN 2018036178 (ebook) |
    ISBN 9781681036649 (ebook) | ISBN 9781626179394 (hardcover : alk. paper)
Subjects: LCSH: Reindeer--Juvenile literature. | Animals--Arctic regions--Juvenile literature.
Classification: LCC QL737.U55 (ebook) | LCC QL737.U55 P484 2019 (print) | DDC 599.65/8--dc23
LC record available at https://lccn.loc.gov/2018030992

Editor: Rebecca Sabelko   Designer: Jeffrey Kollock

Printed in the United States of America, North Mankato, MN

Table of Contents

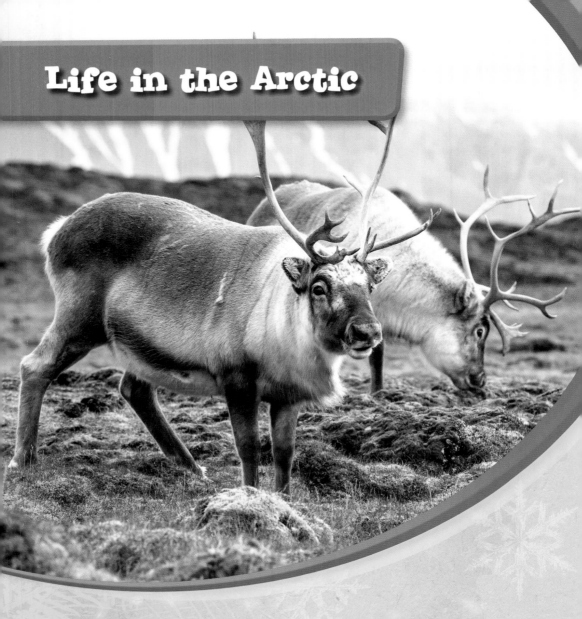

Reindeer live in the cold **taiga** and Arctic **biomes**.

They are found in North America, Europe, and Asia. Reindeer are called caribou in North America.

Reindeer Range

N
W   E
S

range =

Double **coats** keep reindeer warm. Short hairs near the skin trap air and heat.

6

Their outer hairs are **hollow**. These help reindeer stay warm and float in water.

Arctic air is cold. Reindeer have a special bone inside their noses. The bone helps warm the air.

They never have to breathe cold air into their lungs!

Reindeer hooves change with the seasons. Soft hooves in summer help them walk on soft ground.

Special Adaptations

antlers

double coat

hard winter hooves

Their hooves become hard and furry during the winter. This keeps their feet warm.

Reindeer travel great distances in **herds**. Some **migrate** over 600 miles (966 kilometers) north each spring.

They move to feed, have young, and escape **insects** that bite.

Reindeer Stats

Least Concern	Near Threatened	Vulnerable	Endangered	Critically Endangered	Extinct in the Wild	Extinct

conservation status: vulnerable

life span: 10 to 15 years

herd

13

Reindeer begin to move again in the fall. They slowly move south to safe, wooded forests.

They feed and put on fat to get ready for the Arctic winter.

Finding Food

Reindeer are **herbivores**. They eat many different types of plants depending on the season.

They mostly eat **lichens** during the winter.

lichens

antlers

Lichens grow under the deep snow.

Reindeer use their front hooves and **antlers** to dig for this favorite food.

Reindeer Diet

lichens

blueberries

willow leaves

They eat grass, berries, flowers, and leaves in the summer.

The Arctic is a hard place to live. But reindeer have **adapted** to their home!

Glossary

adapted—changed over a long period of time

antlers—branched bones on the heads of some animals; antlers look like horns.

biomes—large areas with certain plants, animals, and weather

coats—the hair or fur covering some animals

herbivores—animals that only eat plants

herds—groups of reindeer that live and travel together

hollow—empty through the middle

insects—small animals with six legs and hard outer bodies; an insect's body is divided into three parts.

lichens—plantlike living things that grow on rocks and trees

migrate—to move from one area to another, often with the seasons

taiga—a wet northern forest that begins where the Arctic ends

To Learn More

AT THE LIBRARY

Best, Arthur. *Reindeer*. New York, N.Y.: Cavendish Square, 2019.

Gagne, Tammy. *Caribou*. Lake Elmo, Minn.: North Star Editions, 2017.

Statts, Leo. *Caribou*. Minneapolis, Minn.: Abdo Zoom, 2017.

ON THE WEB

FACTSURFER

Factsurfer.com gives you a safe, fun way to find more information.

1. Go to www.factsurfer.com.

2. Enter "reindeer" into the search box.

3. Click the "Surf" button and select your book cover to see a list of related web sites.

Index

The images in this book are reproduced through the courtesy of: Michelle Holihan, front cover (reindeer); Incredible Arctic, pp. 4-5; Arildina, pp. 6, 18-19; Bogorodskiy, pp. 6-7; Fufachew Ivan Andreevich, pp. 8-9; Vladimir Melnikov, pp. 9, 11; Pim Leijen, pp. 10-11; Jukka Jantunen, p. 12; Olga Danylenko, pp. 12-13; Evgeniia Ozerkina, pp. 14-15; Ferenc Cegledi, p. 15; Robert Haasmann, p. 16; Tim Greyhavens, pp. 16-17; Zelma Brezinska, p. 19 (lichens); Andris Tkacenko, p. 19 (blueberries); sun_and_moon, p. 19 (willow); Menno Schaefer, p. 20; Joanna Perchaluk, pp. 20-21; Iakov Filimonov, p. 23.